Dedicated To:

My family that I love so much and who has always been supportive!

Table of Contents

Foreword

The main purpose of this small book is to inspire those who have the power in Puerto Rico such as the politicians, private investors, developers and the residents of Puerto Rico to increase their efforts in preserving the rich history of the island. Puerto Rico needs Historic Preservation to restore the former glory to the island that earned it the name "Isla de Encanto." My objective is not to disrepute anyone by saying that exertions have not been made for the betterment of the island, but to point out that there is room for greater economic growth. Historic Preservation is a prodigious tool, but that has not been effectively utilized here on the island other than a few places such as Old San Juan and Ponce for the most part.

I am passionate about the preservation of Puerto Rico because I have traveled many places in the world and no place has captivated me more than this is island, which is where I now call home. I am enamored with the people, the places, the traditions, the beaches, the mountains and the beautiful variety of European architecture that is found throughout this island. I see beauty where others cannot, and I am optimistic that the evidence presented in this book will be sufficient to incite others to take measures that will result in a better economy, greater morale for the people and a healthier, more sustainable environment for the Common Wealth of Puerto Rico.

Introduction

In the past, Historic Preservation might have been thought of as an inconsequential economic development tool. Conversely, city planners, economists and others in the industry now recognize the value that Historic Preservation can bring to local, regional and national economies. The General Assembly of Georgia stated that, *"Historic Preservation, far from being a 'frill' as is sometimes thought, has produced visible and measurable economic development in Georgia communities."*

Downtown Revitalization is the process of using existing resources to restore the downtown area to a diverse center that provides commercial and residential opportunities that produce revenues for a city resulting in an improved quality of life for its Inhabitants and a stronger economy.

Preservation efforts have augmented many economies throughout the United States by creating more commerce, increasing tourism, reducing landfill waste, restoring residences and improving the overall quality of life for the inhabitants of the cities that have utilized Main Street Programs, Downtown Revitalization and other preservation strategies to revive their respective towns. The concept of a *"Downtown Revitalization"* has come to be thought of as one of the most fundamental instruments in reviving a city as a whole; downtown is the heart of a city and without that, the city will not thrive.

As the oldest colony in the world, the built environment in Puerto Rico is heavily influenced by Spanish, French, and American architecture. Many buildings here are hundreds of years old and they tell a story about the development of Puerto Rico as we know it today. These stories should not be forgotten and the structures that house them are assets to the island that attract both tourists and locals seeking to learn about the past. It has already been proven that downtown revitalization is an effective tool that can improve the economy of many pueblos in Puerto Rico; Old San Juan is composed of several historic districts and sites and brings in millions of dollars in revenues each year from *"Historic Tourism"* alone.

Considering that economy of Puerto Rico depends heavily on tourism, one has to ask the question, "Why aren't other areas that offer tourist attractions as popular as Old San Juan?" In the following chapters I will discuss why natural resources such as beaches, the rainforest and outdoor adventure tours are not enough to produce a surplus of revenues and how Historic Preservation will improve Puerto Rico by in more ways than one.

The Economic Crisis in Puerto Rico

Most people are already aware of the fact that Puerto Rico has been in a recession since 2006, but not everyone is aware of the gravity of the situation. One of the most troubling statistic is the fact that **more than 40% of people live below the poverty line in Puerto Rico**, that is nearly twice as much as the state of Mississippi which 24.2% of people living below poverty and is considered the poorest of the United States. To give a clearer perspective on what this means, the Puerto Rico poverty line has been established as a household earning less than $22,881 per year for a family of four; the average household in Puerto Rico only earns $19,429 a year. That calculates out to around $1600 a month before any deductions. This number doesn't even compare to the median household income of the United States of $51,371 that was reported at the end of 2012. It may be difficult for you to even imagine how ta family of four could survive on such little income.

The poverty statistics are a direct reflection of the unemployment rate on the island. **According to the Bureau of Labor and Statistics, the unemployment rate for Puerto Rico in 2013 was 14.7%, no surprise that this number is double the average rate of unemployment in the U.S. for 2013, which was 7.3%.** As distressing as these numbers are, they don't take into account for those who were not reported in the census, nor does it account for those who have ceased looking for employment. On top of it all, Puerto Rico has a debt of more than $70 billion with no prospect of repayment. One has to ask the question, "If people here earn so little, then why are some of the costs of living so high?" Research shows that the average utility costs for a small apartment in New York is $161 a month compared to an average of $246 a month here on the island.

Substandard medical care on the island is also a consequence of the suffering economy in Puerto Rico. More than 90% of people in Puerto Rico are covered by government medical insurance (Medicaid), which at first glance may seem like a good thing, but it has put a severe strain on the Medicaid system. As a result, Medicaid often pays out less than the minimum fees to medical professionals for services rendered to patients forcing doctors to cram as many patients as possible into each day just to earn a salary. Private medical insurance is the only alternative, but the with the cost being so high, it is not affordable for the majority of the population.

The concept of having a scheduled "appointment" at any doctor's office here on the island is fictional at best. A typical visit to the doctor consists of arriving to a clinic around 5:30 a.m. and waiting outside in a line with other patients until the clinic opens, which could be anytime between 6:00 a.m. and 8:00 a.m. Once you are n the clinic, you are lucky if you have a seat to wait for your turn in an overly crowded office. The doctor usually shows up around 10:00 a.m., and the average wait time is

3-6 hours to see the doctor. It doesn't matter if it is a general practice or a specialty clinic, an urgent matter or a routine check up; if you arrive later than 8:00 a.m., chances are you won't be seen at all that day.   Medical procedures such as surgeries are even worse. For a simple out patient surgery, a patient typically has to see 6-7 different doctors to collect superfluous referrals and paperwork prior to approval for even a simple routine outpatient surgery. Then the day after their surgery, patients are typically required to return to the clinic where the surgery was performed and wait another 3-7 hours to be seen regardless of their post-surgery pains and discomfort. This is just an example of how the quality of life is severely impacted in an adverse way due to the economic problems of the island.

With all the issues that currently plague the Puerto Rican economy, it's no wonder that many people, the majority being professionals who migrate to the states in search of better opportunities. The Census Bureau's Community Survey estimates that about 55,000 people have left the island each year for the last three years. This loss of valuable citizens is disastrous for two reasons. The first being that **The Department of Education in Puerto Rico spends an average of $8,000 a year per student only to have them take their skills elsewhere.** The second is that the loss of affluent members of the community only aggravates the problems here by increasing the ratio of uneducated people who depend heavily on government aide on the island.

In an interview on CNN, Puerto Rican political analyst Jay Fonseca said, "*Why invest so much time and money for a student in Puerto Rico only to have them leave to the U.S. and contribute to society elsewhere?*"

With so many economic problems the rate of crime and drug use has increased significantly. A study conducted by Michigan State University indicated that, "*Puerto Rico has a homicide rate of 29/100,000 people which is six times higher than the average homicide rate in the continental United States.*" Regardless of the urgency of the situation, economic experts predict that there will not be a bailout from the United States. This means that the people and the government of Puerto Rico have to take the initiative into their own hands to develop an economic strategy to overcome their financial struggles. The sad reality is that the quality of life in Puerto Rico is approaching a "*third world*" status in some aspects. It is no longer a question of whether or not Puerto Rico is on a downward spiral economically, but what can be done to reverse the situation?

Historic Preservation: *An Economic Tool*

The word "**economy**" can be defined as *"The thrifty and efficient use of material resources: frugality in expenditures."* The municipalities of Puerto Rico have many structures that are abandoned and/or are used inefficiently; this equates to dollars that are not being stretched as far as they can go and that is uneconomical. The preservation or restoration of a neighborhood where an infrastructure already exist with power lines, sewer lines, buildings and roads is much more economical than the developing a new community.

Most cities in the U.S. have begun with the revitalization of their downtown areas since that is considered the heart of the city. *Downtown Revitalization* is the process of using existing resources to restore the downtown area to a diverse center that provides commercial and residential opportunities, which produce revenues for a city, resulting in an improved quality of life for its Inhabitants and a more diversified economy.

One program that has been key to Downtown Revitalization efforts is the Main Street Program (MSP). Many cities, both big and small throughout the United States have utilized the MSP to revitalize their historic districts both downtown and in adjacent communities. The National Trust for Historic Preservation developed the MPS in 1980 to promote the revitalization of downtown areas through a set of established principles that have proven to be efficacious in nearly every downtown area in which it has been employed. **In the year 2012 alone, almost 25,000 new jobs were created & more than 7,000 buildings were rehabilitated within the communities that participated in the MSP.**

Preservation efforts have augmented many economies throughout the United States by creating more commerce, increasing tourism, reducing landfill waste, restoring residences and strengthening the economy; creating an overall better quality of life for its inhabitants. City planners and economists recognize the value that Historic Preservation can bring to local, regional and national economies. The General Assembly of Georgia stated that, "*Historic Preservation, far from being a 'frill' as is sometimes thought, has produced visible and measurable economic development in Georgia communities.*"

Historic Districts Increase Tourism

Historic Districts attract both tourists and locals because of the desire to learn about and experience history. *"Compared to the average trip in the U.S., historically/cultural trips are more likely to be seven nights or longer and include air travel, a rental car, and a hotel stay. Historic/cultural travelers are also more likely to extend their stay to experience history and culture at their destination. In fact, four in ten added extra time to their trip specifically because of a historic/cultural activity."*

In addition to increased tourism, the designation of a downtown area as a Historic District can mean more efficient use of dollars. Buildings that are registered as historic or part of a historic district may qualify for a tax credit of up to 20% and in some cases, this credit may also be combined with the Low Income Housing Tax Credit. *"For the five most recent years, (FY99-FY03) over half of the projects receiving the historic rehabilitation tax credit have cost less than $500,000 with an average of 17% being less than $100,000."* It is evident that the implementation of Historic Preservation helps to progress an economy.

Some people may fear that the enforcement of historic zone restrictions drive away developers. On the contrary, many developers have worked very closely with city planning committees to arrive at solutions that profitable, yet satisfy the needs of the city. Furthermore, areas designated as Historic Districts attract investors because as mentioned before, incentives decrease their overall investment making their projects even more profitable.

Let's take a look at how a Historic District could enhance tourism in Rio Grande, the city that houses the National Rainforest of Puerto Rico. Despite the fact that the *"Yunque"* is a major tourist attraction, there are very little revenues generated from tourism. The majority of tourism revenues in Rio Grande go to the three major resorts in Rio Grande: The Coco Beach Hotel & Golf Resort, The St. Regis Luxury Resort and the Wyndham Rio Mar. The reason is that after tourists visit the rainforest, there are no other attractions in the town, so they either drive back to San Juan or go back to their resort where they spend the majority of their money.

The resorts contribute to the local economy by creating jobs, but many of the employees only earn a decent living during the "high" season and the remainder of the year they earn little to no wages. The town center has little to offer as a tourist attraction and so local businesses struggle to remain open. The resorts capitalize on this situation by providing "activity clubs", golf and restaurants on their properties that make it convenient for guests, eliminating the desire for them to explore anything outside of the property.

The town of Luquillo, which is to the east of Rio Grande, is another tourist town that could benefit from the creation of a Historic District. Tourists as well as locals of the island can enjoy soft, "family friendly" waves with access to ideal surf conditions a few blocks away. The "kioscos," is another popular attraction of the town, which is located along the shoreline. A variety of food and drinks including alcoholic beverages can be enjoyed just a few steps from the water at very reasonable prices and many of the kiosks even provide live music on the weekends. Unlike Rio Grande, no major resorts exist here, most travelers' stay in condominiums along the beach that are rented out by private owners. The great thing about Luquillo is that its "pueblo" or town center already has the infrastructure of a "walkable" community. Local eateries such as William's Pizza, Aromas & Eric's Gyro & Deli just to name a few provide a quaint charm to the area, but there still exist a vast amount of vacant buildings going to ruins. The establishment of a Historic District in the town center, along with the restoration of some of the vacant properties would increase tourism to the area and increase revenues for local business owners as well as property values.

One of the busiest marinas on the island is directly east of Luquillo and is home to the Conquistador Resort & Casino. Nearly all boats traveling to the island of Vieques, Icacos, Culebras, St. Thomas & St. Croix depart from Fajardo. The town is also popular for it's water activities such snorkeling, scuba diving and bioluminescence bay excursions. Despite all that Fajardo has to offer as a tourist destination,

the dilapidated appearance of the town center and adjacent areas is

uninviting to tourists. Just like Rio Grande and Luquillo, Fajardo has the

potential to gain so much more revenue from tourism if the area were

better preserved and offered historic attractions.

Even if an entire Historic District isn't established, historic sites scattered throughout a city can still be effective in promoting tourism. In Old San Juan, the **Fortaleza** has been converted into a museum where visitors can walk freely through the fort and see the original sleeping quarters, uniforms and artillery rooms of the Conquistadors. Visitors appreciate the learning experience as they visit each area and read about the historical relevance of each exhibit. A gift store conveniently located at the end of the tour gives tourists the opportunity to spend more dollars on souvenirs, literature about Puerto Rico, and artwork from local artisans. Each year tourist and island locals visit and stay in Old San Juan where they spend millions of dollars that go to towards the cities annual revenues. In 2011, the state of Puerto Rico earned $61,000,000 from national park tourism proving that there is value in historic attractions here on the island. Why else would so many people visit Old San Juan each year? There's no golf, exceptional beaches, rainforest or other major attractions... just history.

Other municipalities in Puerto Rico have the potential to gain just

as much by emphasizing their historic possessions as Old San Juan, if not

more; a little effort can bring out a lot of beauty. A representative from

the city of Galveston, TX said, "*While Galveston's sun and ocean beaches*

have long attracted tourists, it is apparent that the city's historic

attractions are making a substantial contribution to the local

economy." Each region of Puerto Rico is beautiful in its own way, but the

key here is to give tourists more than one reason to visit a town, entice

them to stay longer and provide educational experiences that appeal to

more than just the leisure traveler.

Older Buildings Are Assets, Not Liabilities

Here in Puerto Rico, there are countless single and multi-family homes along with entire apartment buildings that have been abandoned; these properties should be seen as assets, not liabilities. If funds, time and care were invested into these properties then it would enhance the value of the communities in which they exist.

Older buildings are resources to a community which when utilized properly can provide new jobs, housing, and promote local business. It has been proven that restoration projects put more money back into the local community than new construction developments. The average restoration project delegates 60% - 70% of the budget towards labor as compared to new construction projects that budget about 50% for labor and the other half for materials.

The need for local architects, engineers, contractors, laborers and artisans will create new job openings within the community and those who are employed will in turn spend a portion of their wages at eateries, banks, retail stores and other local businesses. It is also likely to find materials that are appropriate for a restoration project locally, therefore the majority of the remaining 30% - 40% of the budget will also be returned to the local economy. New construction methods often require vast amounts of materials that are only available from distant locations, so the majority of the materials budget is usually spent outside of the local economy.

Older buildings are ideal for small business owners because they offer a variety of sizes and; buildings that are built with newer construction methods, and often on grids restrict layout and size configurations. As more buildings become available through rehabilitation efforts, small businesses will relocate to the neighborhood and create new jobs; research shows that small businesses are responsible for more new jobs each year than large corporations.

The restoration of residential dwellings is equally as beneficial for the economy as restoring commercial spaces, especially in a downtown area. Commercial buildings convey the vision of older times in a historic district and provide a feeling of financial livelihood, but residential dwellings such as homes and apartments are what give a neighborhood charm.

Large buildings are typically limited to certain architectural styles that lend themselves to grand scale construction and formality. Take for instance the fact that many state buildings in the United States are built in the Federal style; a favorite of Thomas Jefferson because it utilizes classical styling and proportions. Houses and multi-family units were designed with fewer restrictions and most were intended to accommodate the needs of individual families and the owner's personal preferences. Here in Puerto Rico, most residences are influenced by Spanish, Art Deco & Prairie style architecture.

The restoration and designation of one historic building can be the catalyst to begin other developments within the vicinity. Historic Preservation has been proven to stabilize, and in many cases, increase the property values of a neighborhood. Historic districts often attract more affluent people to the neighborhood, creating a healthy mix of families with various income levels. Research shows that as the number of vacant properties decrease so does crime. Less vacancies also equal more tax revenues and an increase in property values that influence private investors and other homeowners to improve their properties.

In some cases, the designation of a neighborhood as a historic district is unwelcomed because fear exist that current residents in the lower income brackets will be forced out of the neighborhood. However, gentrification does not have to occur when the community is properly planned. Older homes may offer a more affordable cost of living than newer homes constructed in urban developments. The majority of older homes were constructed with thicker walls made from concrete, stone or other masonry materials that provide greater insulation from hot and cold weather, significantly reducing utility bills as compared to newer homes.

Older apartment buildings should be considered a jewel to developers, investors and government agencies. Due to the fact that older apartment buildings may need extensive work, they can be purchased for low prices and restored for lower costs than new construction; this allows building owners to provide housing at lower rent amounts and still gain a profit on their investment. Likewise, government agencies could stretch tax dollars further by rehabilitating older buildings for low-income housing programs such as section 8 and senior living facilities.

When older buildings are abandoned and allowed to become dilapidated, they directly affect the property values of the neighborhood in a deleterious manner. An analysis by the National Association of Home Builders found that *abandoned buildings could reduce home prices by more than 30% percent.* Abandoned buildings also result in the loss of affluent members of a community, a rise in crime and the loss of local businesses.

When a neighborhood reflects a pitiable image, it is a welcome sign for the delinquent members of society to take over. This flagrant irresponsibility to the citizens of a community must cease; the local governments, along with property and business owners must do their part to preserve their neighborhoods. The former mayor of Boston Thomas Menino once said, *"You can't have a center of neighborhood and have vacancies and no vitality and expect people to have confidence in that neighborhood."*

Preservation Is Better For The Eco-System

Historic Preservation is not just about improving the economy or turning a profit; it also protects ecosystems. The truth is that the entire world, including Puerto Rico has to figure out a more ecologically friendly way to house the growing population. The creation of infinite new housing developments and high rises is not the answer to a growing population. No matter how efficient the design, even the "greenest" buildings still consumed more energy and create more pollution in their creation than using what already existed. Historic Preservation is an efficient tool that can be used to implement the two most important "R's" of the environment, which are "reduce" and "reuse."

Reduce. The calamitous fact is that many people in the world have been conditioned to have a greater appreciation for things that are bigger, better and newer. Developers profit with the construction of each new high-rise, track home development and corporate skyscraper building; contributing to the insatiable mentality of consumers. These new projects only injure the ecosystems in which they are built by producing more waste that will go to landfills. How much waste is created when an older building is demolished to make way for a new one? It is no surprise that the construction industry is one of, if not the greatest contributors to waste on the planet every year.

In the case of Puerto Rico, or any other island, land is limited and even greater care should be taken to reduce waste and protect the environment. So why do the governing officials in Puerto Rico continue to permit developers to construct new buildings instead of encouraging them through incentives to rehabilitate existing ones?

It is time to reduce the amount of energy and materials that are consumed on the island. There is a surplus of vacant residential and commercial buildings in every pueblo of Puerto Rico, buildings that can be rehabilitated to accommodate new needs. Reducing the consumption of new materials is the most effective way to prevent further damage to the ecosystem and create a more sustainable environment. We also have to look at ways to reduce our carbon footprints. Although it is alluring to build more homes in the suburbs with 300 square foot master bedrooms, is it really necessary? The inventory already exist, we just need to use it.

Reuse. A developer can only build what the city allows; city planning committees need to be erected to evaluate the needs of each town and provide guidance to developers. The reuse of existing buildings will greatly reduce the need for demolition and new materials, producing less waste to go to landfills on the island. The reuse of existing structures is one of the most fundamental things we as humans can do for the Earth.

The Life Cycle Assessment (LCA) method is recognized worldwide as a tool to analyze a building and it's materials through six stages to determine its impact on the environment and human health. The LCA uses six stages to analyze a project: extraction, transformation, manufacture, distribution, use and end of life.

The *extraction* stage is when a raw material is removed from its natural environment such as a tree being cut down or granite being mined. Even the harvesting of "eco-friendly" materials requires energy; energy that could have been saved by reusing what already existed. The next stage is *transformation*, where more energy is used as chemical treatments, and various machines are required to refine raw materials. In the *manufacture* stage, more energy is consumed as materials are assembled and packaged for shipping to suppliers. Packaging is another issue that arises with new materials and also contributes to landfill waste. In the *distribution* stage, materials are shipped to a building site. How much energy is used in this stage, especially on an island where everything must be shipped in? Up until this point, an existing building has had very little, if any additional impact on the environment; the energy needed to extract, transform, manufacture and transport the majority of the building products has already been accounted for.

The first four stages of a LCA shows the impact of a product on a global scale, but as the product reaches the building site these products, and projects they were intended for, begin to impact the local environment. The *use* stage of the LCA takes into consideration the energy needed for construction as well as the energy that will be consumed for operations through the life of the building. The materials and energy consumed to restore a building is less than what is required for ground up construction. Many newer building are designed to be energy efficient and will consume less energy in operating costs, but older buildings can be fitted with new technologies that will make them just as, if not more efficient.

The End of Life stage is the final analysis in the LCA method. It analyzes the amount of energy that will be consumed to dispose of building materials when it is no longer deemed useful. This stage also considers the effect it will have on landfills and whether or not any of the materials are capable of being recycled. When an older building is replaced by a newer one, a massive amount of waste material will go to a landfill upon the demolition of the older building and another mass will go to the landfill 30-40 years from now. Leaders in the construction industry predict that newer structures are built to last an average of 30-50 years compared to mature buildings that last 100 years or more due to the older construction methods.

We have to reuse the assets that we already have; newer is not always better. France is a great example of a country that capitalizes on the value of their historic buildings instead of tearing them down or letting them become dilapidated. Instead, they preserve, restore and rehabilitate older buildings to give them purpose again. Materials can also be reclaimed from other buildings, which might be otherwise hard to find. An example might be a case where demolition is the only option for an old structure; prior to demolition, the building should be surveyed for useful materials that can be used for other projects.

As a result of the disinterest in existing neighborhoods and the irresponsibility of those who grant building permits, **urban sprawl** is becoming problematic in Puerto Rico. Urban sprawl is, *"The spreading of urban developments (as houses and shopping centers) on undeveloped land near a city."* The extent to which the geography of Puerto Rico is exploited is shameful. Who benefits from the investors who are continually carving away the mountains for new developments? Heavy developments along the shorelines take away from the natural habitat, increase pollution on the beaches and in the water and impede views. The exploitation of natural environments is increasingly creating a negative impact on the ecosystem of Puerto Rico, and for many is considered a desecration of the island.

The construction of new buildings in areas that are remotely located from city centers destroy natural animal habitats and the delicate balance of the ecosystem. **Rainwater run-off pollution** increases as grassy areas are replaced with concrete and other non-absorbent surfaces. In addition to the structures themselves, additional infrastructure to provide roads, water and electrical to the new development are usually required, which increase the amount of waste and pollution produced by new developments. Residents that are located in isolated areas must drive additional distances for their everyday commute's; this coupled with the reduction of trees greatly increases air pollution.

It is not a crime to live in the *suburbs*, and it's understandable why these areas are appealing. Some families prefer the low-density lifestyle that offers larger homes with more spacious yards at lower prices. Many seek a more prosperous neighborhood when downtown areas and city centers have been neglected and harbor more criminal activity. Others prefer the scenery that a beachfront condo or a house on the top of a mountain offers. I'm not saying that I resent anyone who wants to live away from the city, nor should they be prohibited from pursuing their dream home wherever it may be located. In fact, I live at the edge of the rainforest myself for all three of the above reasons. What I am saying is that there is a huge inventory of homes and apartments to choose from, so there is no need to build new structures. Homeowners and developers should not be anxious about older structures, renovations can be very profitable, and it gives way for the opportunity to customize many aspects of a home. It is true that a renovation project can be costly and time consuming, but it is still a better alternative than new construction and will increase the value of the property and the neighborhood in which it resides.

Conclusion

Historic Preservation is a tool that has been used for decades in the United States and hundreds of years in older regions of the world such as Europe. Puerto Rico can also realize improvement in its economy through the restoration, rehabilitation and preservation of its current assets. The island already offers beautiful beaches, rainforests, rivers and other attractions that draw tourist here from around the world. However, the economic hardship that has blanketed the island is proof that it is not enough to prevent more than 40% of the population from living beneath the poverty line. Historic Preservation is not the "end all" answer to an economic dilemma, but it is a great place to begin the rebuilding of an island that has the potential to thrive economically.

In addition to improving the economy, greater preservation efforts will help the island become more sustainable. One of the most alluring qualities of the island is the multitude of flora, and fauna that are native to the island; many of which will cease to exist if the ecosystem is not protected. The quantity of waste and pollution that is generated yearly by new construction is unjustified due to the vast inventory of existing buildings that exist on every part of the island. The best method to provide more housing and new commercial opportunities is to restore existing buildings.

I believe that overall, the most important reasons to increase Historic Preservation efforts in Puerto Rico is to improve the morale and the quality of life of the people. The fact that over 50,000 people have left the island each year for the past three years is a desperate cry for help that must be answered. I think that greater Historic Preservation efforts would bring a renewed since of pride, opportunities and interest to the island that would improve the economy, increase tourism and encourage affluent professionals to return to the island.

After investigating the results of other cities that have used Historic Preservation as a tool to improve their economies, I have no doubt that Puerto Rico can do the same. In addition to the economic benefits, Historic Preservation contributes to a more sustainable way of life that will help preserve the natural beauty of the island and maintain a healthy environment for years to come. The bottom line is that if Historic Preservation is implemented in the proper way, it can only result in the betterment of Puerto Rico!

Citations

I.   Figure 1. (Cover) – Scott, Shayna. "Abandoned Apartments. Downtown Rio Grande." Rio Grande. 2014. Jpeg.

II.   *"Economy."* Merriam-Webster's Collegiate Dictionary. 2014. Web. 10March2014.

III.   Guzman, Timothy Alexander. "US Hegemony and Puerto Rico's Economic Crisis." *Global Research* 17 December 2013: *Silent Crow News.* Web. 27 March 2014.

IV.   Rodriguez, Cindy Y. "Why more Puerto Ricans are living in mainland U.S. than in Puerto Rico." *CNN 24* March 2014: *CNN Global News View.* Web. 28 March 2014.

V.   CB Online Staff. "Census: PR poverty up, income down." *Caribbean Business PR.* Caribbean Business, 23 September 2012. Web. 19 March 2014.

VI.   Mead, Kevin. "PR population below 3.7M; income, poverty hold." *Caribbean Business PR.* Caribbean Business, 20 September 2013. Web. 19 March 2014

VII.   Rypkema, Donovan D. *The Economics of Historic Preservation: A Community Leader's Guide.* Washington, D.C.: The National Trust for Historic Preservation, 1994. Print.

VIII.   Boudonck, Greg. *Rio Grande, Puerto Rico: Ciudad de El Yunque.* Lexington: G.L. Boudonck, 2012. Print.

IX.   Tyler, Norman. *Historic Preservation: An Introduction to Its History, Principles, and Practice.* New York: W.W. Norton & Company, 2000. Print.

X.   "Rio Grande." Puerto Rico Encyclopedia. Puerto Rico: Fundación Puertorriqueña de Las Humanidades, 2014. Web. 11 March. 2014.

XI.   United States. National Park Service. *Tax Credit Basics.* 2014. Web. 11 March 2014.

XII.   *Report of the Joint Study Committee: Economic Development through Historic Preservation.* The General Assembly, State of Georgia, 1987.

XIII.   Rivera, Magaly. "Rio Grande." *Welcometopuertorico.com.* Welcome To Puerto Rico, 2014. Web. 05 March. 2014.

XIV.   Federal Tax Incentives for Rehabilitating Historic Buildings: Statistical Report and Analysis for fiscal year 2003.

XV.   United States. National Trust for Historic Preservation. *2012 Yearly Reinvestment Statistics: The Main Street Programs Economic Success.* Unknown. 2014. Web. 10 March 2014.

XVI.   United States. National Park Service. *Working with Puerto Rico.* 2014. Web. 12 March 2014.

XVII.   Joni Leithe, Thomas Muller, John Petersen & Susan Robinson. *The Economic Benefits of Preserving Community Character, A Case Study:* Galveston, TX. Chicago: Government Finance Officers Association, 1991.

XVIII. National Association of Home Builders, "Location, Neighborhood

Most Important Factors When Buying a Home," Housing News

Service. Press Release, December 2, 1993.

XIX. United States. National Institute of Building Science. *Sustainable

Historic Preservation.* Whole Building Design Guide Historic

Preservation Subcommittee, 02Dec 2013. Web. 09 April 2014.

XX. *"Urban Sprawl."* Merriam-Webster's Collegiate Dictionary. 2014.

Web. 11 Apr 2014.

XXI. Brody, S. "The Characteristics, Causes, and Consequences of

Sprawling Development Patterns in the United States." *Nature

Education Knowledge.* 2013. Web. 11 Apr 2014.

XXII. United States. National Library of Medicine. *Urban Sprawl, Smart
Growth, and Deliberative Democracy.* Resnik, David B., PhD, Oct 2010. Web.
23 Mar 2014.

XXIII. Cooper, Rachel. "Tudor Place Historic House And Garden: A

Historic House Museum in Georgetown." *About.com.* 2014. Web.

16 March 2014.

XXIV. "Taste of Chicago." *Wikipedia.* City of Chicago. 27 February 2014.

Web. 16 March 2014.

XXV. United States. Natural Resources Defense Council. *The 3R's Still

Rule.* Eisenberg, Sheryl, Feb. 2008. Web. 07 Apr 2014.

XXVI. Figure 2. (Back Cover) – Scott, Shayna. "Isla de Icacos." Fajardo.

2013. Jpeg.

www.ingramcontent.com/pod-product-compliance
Lightning Source LLC
Chambersburg PA
CBHW021856170526
45157CB00006B/2479